Redefining Me:

Lessons Learned in the Refiner's Fire

Takhia Gaither

The Ready Write-Her
Baltimore, MD

Disclaimer:

This book is not intended as a substitute for the medical advice of physicians and/or licensed counselors and therapists. The reader should consult a physician in matters relating to his/her mental health and particularly with respect to any symptoms that may require diagnosis or medical attention.

ISBN (Print): 979-8-9881944-2-2
ISBN (Digital): 979-8-9881944-3-9
Library of Congress Number: 2023907706

Printed in the United States of America

DEDICATION

To the countless women who have lived or may be living your own version of any part of these stories, you're not alone. May the words on these pages strengthen, encourage, and remind you that you are loved, you are heard, and if you feel that no one else sees or understands you, know that I do.

TABLE OF CONTENTS

ACKNOWLEDGMENTS

There are so many people to thank and while I would love to type out a list like they do with all the movie extras, I don't want to leave anyone out. So, to that end, I will say find your group or groups that you fit into, smile big, and tell people, my best-selling author _____ (fill in the blank with your relationship) is talking to me! Here we go, on to the Grammy list!

Thank You, Jesus!!!!!!!!! For all the things, all the time, and for the ways, You always allow my gifts to make room for me. Thank You doesn't do it just, I am forever grateful.

To my 4 – as a mother, we have to make a lot of on-the-spot decisions that not only affect us but you as well. There's a lot I wish you never had to see or experience but knowing that you were watching me, from the youngest to the oldest, is a big part of what brought my fight back to me. You're all growing up to be phenomenal people and I'm so proud of each of you. I love you forever! Xoxo

To my parents, John & Valeria, to my Gert, my brother-in-love, the Rats, the fabulous Baker boys (Uncles and Cousins), my not-so-little-anymore sisters, and the Bakers, Gaithers, Hammonds, Blackstones, and Hodges (man

I hope I got everybody!) - I don't have enough words to say thank you. For listening, for praying, for being ready to tie up boots (lol), for always reminding me, who I am. Love you!!!

To my friends who are really extensions of my family, my sisters, near and far, new and old, in-person and online, the laughs, the cries, the advice (solicited or not), the layouts, for being not just my friends but my sisters. Talk every day or on the fly, it is always good to know that if I send out the bat signal, y'all are right there. Love you!!

To Pastor and Lady Rowson and the Kingdom Nation family, thank you for never letting me be "just a visitor." If you ever need proof of the mission being fulfilled, it's me. For the last 4 years, you have definitely loved me to life as I was on this path to destiny.

To my up-and-coming author and sister friend, Patricia E. Pritchette, thank you for lending your editing eye to my work! And for all of the support and encouragement through as we always say "all the things!"

FOREWORD

This literary body of work is a powerful example of the resilience and tenacity of women. Page after page, the author fearlessly reveals her strength and vulnerability by walking the reader through her personal journey of brokenness, healing, and self-awakening. She used her most intimate and potentially devastating life's experiences as a springboard to a greater sense of purpose, revelation, and **redefining**. Each chapter unfolds the lessons learned and steps needed to live in the abundance of peace and joy that God desires for all of us.

As an experienced educator, lifelong learner, and a sold out committed follower of Jesus Christ, it's no surprise that the author would take what she's learned and pen this series of proverbial lesson plans to help others navigate through life's highs and lows. As I read each word, I became increasingly overwhelmed with joy and relief as I began to reflect. You see, I had the fortunate but unfortunate benefit of closely seeing many of the moments discussed in this book unfold in real time. I watched and fervently prayed as she humbly yielded and allowed God (the Refiner) to turn up the heat! I saw Him cut, prod, shake up, dismantle, and rebuild her entire life. It wasn't easy, but as you will learn as you read, it was absolutely necessary.

Many of the moments revealed could have resulted in a very different outcome had it not been for God's love and protection. As you read this beautiful depiction of God's grace, you too will appreciate those weighted lessons learned from the refining and re-defining power of God's love.

- *Lady Sheri Rowson*
Kingdom Nation Church & Ministries, Baltimore, MD

INTRODUCTION

My favorite math words and concepts are aleph null, undefined, and infinity. Undefined is so cool, there isn't even a symbol for it, you literally write the word undefined if that's the answer you get. I guess I should also mention that while these are my favorite math words, outside of aleph null, they are usually not the answers you want to get for any problem, except maybe infinity, infinity can be good, but I digress. Switching to Computer Science, having undefined variables results in crashed programs or infinite loops. In either case, there will be delays in your program running and will produce garbage output.

Knowing these things, I still thought it was "fun" to apply them to my life. Especially undefined. It was my way of saying you couldn't put me in a box, I was not a cookie cutter. I was partially right. But undefined also means without definition, i.e., no shape, no meaning, unclear. Although I was wearing undefined as a banner, I was setting myself up for the meanest, biggest, most magnanimous fail ever.

For a relatively smart girl, I made some dumb choices. This is not one of those "Oh, don't be so hard on yourself moments." This is a reality that I had to face. The thing about being a logical thinker is that I can logically present an argument for most things, including and not limited to my own actions and mindsets. Where grace came in was to rescue me from me. When I got to the bottom of what I was beginning to see were problems, there was me waving, saying "Hey girl, hey!" Adopting the attitude of being undefined was the smartest dumb decision ever! While it set the stage for everything that came next and produced some pretty turbulent events, I take nothing for my journey because it built me. God never wastes anything. So, if you're reading right now from a place of wondering if you've made smart dumb moves, you have. What you have also done is made the path for God to use all your things to set you in your purpose.

Redefining Me was and is an ongoing event. Grab a pen, a journal, and a highlighter because we're going on a journey. You'll want notes, not about me, but about where you're going! Let's get into it!

LESSON 1
Xenon

L et's take a brief trip into the world of chemistry. Xenon is a member of the noble gas family that is colorless and odorless. It is known to be inert, meaning it's usually unreactive so it does not normally participate in chemical reactions, nor does it form new compounds. Xenon is a very stable gas on its own because it has a full set of valence electrons. Chemical reactions happen when atoms do not have full sets of valence electrons, so they will bond with the atoms from another element to form a complete set. Xenon's already full, (i.e., complete), set allows it to be comfortable on its own. Now I know everyone is not a science freak and this may sound completely boring and out of place in a book about redefining me but allow me to explain.

Growing up, (and even now), I was strange. Definitely weird. 100% a nerd. Always the smart girl. What I wasn't, was always proud of it. In high school, I had nerd friends, we were all headed somewhere, and it was easy to be ok with being the weird one. At church, we were all in bible study together, got baptized, and holy ghost filled in our teens, and even though I was always on the list of the smart ones (for Sunday school and anything else), it was still ok to be weird me. But then came college ... Life starts to look a little different when the support system you've always leaned on isn't in your face every day. What I began to learn quickly was that churchy (or plain), smart girls with glasses, who were engineering majors rarely got asked on dates. Well, I, ME, MYSELF rarely got asked on dates. Even the boys in the engineering groups seemed to flock to the girls who weren't. There is no lonelier feeling than being in a crowd of people but feeling and sometimes actually being alone. (Which in hindsight, was just really odd and should have been a flag, because I've always been fine being alone and not in or a part of the group. I marched to my own beat.) But it was the wanting to fit in, combined with being away from home that suddenly made me feel that it wasn't ok to be different. I was always the square peg trying to fit into the circle opening.

Things changed in my junior year when I learned that I was a high commodity among men who weren't originally from the United States. But it wasn't because I was cute or smart or even a great person. It was because I had a figure. I was the chunky version of a Brickhouse! Everything else about me was a bonus. I had brains, beauty, and booty! They could take me home to at least the men in the family, (don't get me started on mothers!). By the end of the first semester, I'd met someone who thought the world of me. Everything was great until about 2 years later when it just wasn't. One day according to him, I was too dramatic. Now sidebar, during that particular semester I'd had surgery on my dominant hand and was still recovering, my grandfather passed away the day before I had to go home to have the cast removed, and at the same time my grandmother had just undergone surgery to remove cancer and was about to begin treatment, I was grieving some other events of life and in my SENIOR year, I was failing 2 of the 4 classes that I needed to graduate. With all of that, I think I was entitled to be a little "dramatic." My life was going through drastic change at unprecedented rates and here I was listening to this dude tell me, "You're a wonderful person. You've been there for me. You're my best friend. Let's stay friends." At the time when I needed him the most, the person who was claiming to be my best friend was leaving me to deal with life, and all its issues, alone. And then the twins set in. Rejection and Insecurity. And they hit hard. It was the second time that I'd been dumped at a pivotal time of my life and I could not understand why.

If I have never been anything else in life, I've always been resilient, and this situation was no different. In the words of my grandfather "To heck with him," (But of course he didn't say heck!). I pushed past my feelings with the help of family and friends. I focused on graduating and being the best me that I could be. And that's just what I did. Secretly, I attributed the fall of the relationship to my ambition. I'd always speculated that things came to an end because it was more than apparent that I was going to graduate that May and he wasn't. In his culture, the woman could achieve but never at the expense of or seemingly before, the man. After failing in general, (those 2 classes delayed my degree, I had to move back home, I had no job after graduation and the list goes on), I decided that my ambition and my intelligence were too much. So, I hid them. In meeting a new guy, I would highlight my job as a bank teller, only talk about school if they asked, (I'd just started a master's program) and I was just going to focus on being the cute curvy girl but make all my moves in silence. I hardly even mentioned church, although I made it a point to attend more than I did not, still participated in a few events, and still whole-heartedly loved

God, but steadily ignored many of the things He'd been saying to me! All of that was great until I felt the call to become a teacher. My primary reason for my choice of occupation was because I was tired of seeing brilliant girls dumb themselves down for a boy. Yet here I was doing the very same thing that bothered me about them. I have always been a huge proponent of not being a hypocrite and practicing what I preached, I knew I needed to walk in the confidence that I wanted my female students to have. So, I had a pep talk with myself. I stood in the mirror and said this is for the birds! And in the words of Jay-Z, "this can't be life, this can't be love, there's got to be more." At that moment, God said, "You're absolutely right. Now let's get to work!!"

I needed to become Xenon. Being Xenon did not mean that I needed to be colorless, unseen, and non-bonded. Nor did it mean that I needed to develop the attitude that I'm an island and can stand by myself because I'm all I got. Being Xenon meant that I needed to understand that I was complete by myself and stand on it. I had to remind myself that I have a full set of electrons. My completeness lies in knowing that I am God's precious daughter. He covers me, He protects me, He completes me because in Him I am complete. I am comfortable on my own and in my own self. I have a full set of electrons.

How did I do that? I'm glad you asked. Let's go to Colossians 2:7-10. It gives us a step-by-step guide. **Teacher tip: I am paraphrasing and shortening!! Go read the whole passage for yourself!! ***

Step 1: Colossians 2:7 says to let your roots grow down into Him and let your life be built on Him. Be like the tree, rooted and grounded and unmoving, (Jeremiah 17:8). To grow your roots in Him, read the word. Study it and pray over what you are reading for clarity and insight. As much as this is the digital age, I suggest getting a notebook/journal, your favorite pen, and write these things down. Write your questions, what stands out, and your thoughts in general. Even if you use the digital version, take full advantage of the highlight and note features. Write it all down and revisit it from time to time to see your growth and/or to get new revelations.

Step 2: Colossians 2:8 – the A-clause. Don't let anyone capture you with empty philosophies and high-sounding nonsense that come with human thinking. Two things here. Number 1, people's opinions about you, are not your business. If they choose to share it, you don't have to accept it. Especially when said opinion goes against the things that you know God has called you to be. Number 2, if your circle is full of those people then it's time to find a new circle. See, many of my friends from my youth are still my friends today because throughout the years of other people's thoughts, they always reminded me to be who I was and be ok with it. Surround yourself with people who will encourage you, stretch you, and pray for you. Do not accept anyone else's limitations of you and on you. We serve a limitless God. When they want to impose their doubts or limits on you with all the "why you need to do that?" Or "Well I got this far and I'm good." Thank them for their input and go on about your way. In the words of Rocco "You just do you, Imma do me." (I'm sorry y'all, I haven't been quite delivered from the spirit of hip hop yet... but I digress). Keep in mind that everyone who questions you is not anti-you or against you or "hatin." But this is also where you need to seek discernment. For those who care about you, the questions are to point out things that you may not see or have not considered. It's for them to get on the same page with you and support your efforts. That may come with caution, but it will not come with doubts.

Step 3: Colossians 2:8, the B-clause. Don't let anyone capture you with empty philosophies and high-sounding nonsense that come from the spiritual powers of this world rather than from Christ. Put 2 Corinthians 2:5 into action. Cast down imaginations and everything that exalts itself against the knowledge of God and bring every thought into captivity. Make it a point to constantly work to renew your mind. In today's colloquialisms, stop speaking negative affirmations about and over yourself. Life and death are in the power of YOUR tongue, (Proverbs 18:21). Speak the word of the Lord over yourself. Remind yourself of who He says you are.

Step 4: Now walk it out and claim who you are, by Colossians 2:9-10. You have to know and stand on the fact that in Christ lived the fullness of God in a human body and that you are also complete through your union with Christ, and He is the Lord over EVERYTHING. You are complete. You are whole by yourself. You are exactly who He made you to be. And even if you don't feel like you are, right at this moment, it's ok. You are His. His plans are always for your good and never for your harm (Jeremiah 29:11). Whatever you feel you lack, it's in Him. Press in, lean in, pray in, and receive the love of the Father.

Replace your heaviness with praise and walk in His completeness.

Now listen, I am far from perfect. I still walk through this daily. Some days it seems like by the minute. But I can tell you it all began with a clear decision and that decision was to become who God called me to be no matter what. Becoming a teacher changed many things about the trajectory of my life, but it was only the beginning. I began to boldly and proudly let my smart be known. The response to "what do you do," went from "Oh I'm just a bank teller," to, "I teach math and I'm pursuing a master's degree in Information Technology." And then I'd wait for either the look of shock and amazement or the one that said, "oh snap she's smart." Admittedly, it became funny to see the expressions change as they would politely end conversations and go on their way. At the time though, despite my newfound mission to live out my dream of becoming my own version of Wonder Woman, I had a weakness, (as most superheroes do) - the attention of men who appeared to accept me for my smart and validated it but secretly wanted to crush it. Overcoming that hurdle is a whole book in itself, but what I can tell you today is that beyond a shadow of a doubt, I do not need the validation of others to complete me. My completeness lies in knowing that I am God's precious daughter. He covers me. He protects me. He completes me because in Him I am complete. I am comfortable on my own and in my own self. I know that I have a full set of electrons. I no longer live for or look for reactions.

Allow me to reintroduce myself. Hello, nice to meet you, **I am Xenon**! And the day I embraced that was the day that my narrative began to change.

LESSON 2
His Will or Mine: Only One Could Be Done

I've always been a pretty together person. When things happened, I would step back, evaluate, and come back with a plan to move forward or just be done with whatever it was altogether. This method worked with relationships too. If something was off, uncalled for, ridiculous, or absurd, I was out with a quickness! At some point, I may have been told to or maybe I just thought that I should ease up on people; meet them where they were and love them through it. And while that was admirable, it was also where I should've made a left at Albuquerque! (Does anyone remember that from Bugs Bunny cartoons??)

Today there are countless books, sermons, social media lives, YouTube videos, singles conferences, etc. all warning against the infamous counterfeit. When I was growing up, we were simply given a list of things to avoid combined with the adamant claim "Because God said so." However, walking through life, that only "worked" on things that were direct and blatant. You know, things like, don't do drugs because your body is a temple (and nobody wants to walk around looking like an addict), or don't steal because in getting caught your punishment might involve jail. And finally, you clearly would NOT date a guy who had no regard for God, church, or even you. I don't recall being warned about undercovers and coverts, i.e., people who faked those things very well. It was only said to not be unequally yoked, which was great but what did it really mean? In my naivety, I thought it just meant that he should be willing to go to church to learn and develop his own relationship with God. That worked out well for my parents and it was a decent enough belief, but it was completely inaccurate.

I'm a bit of an empath. I will feel your pain of wanting to grow and if you're committed to growth, then I will do what I can to help you meet your goal. It's a huge part of what my students and other young people I work with say make me a great teacher. Being ok with being the helper and armed with my flawed belief, it was no surprise that I didn't readily see the red flags when I met someone who just couldn't seem to catch a break in life although he was sweet, mannerly, nice, and professed to love God. I figured, at the very least, we'll be friends and I'll help him find his way back to the Lord. I knew he was interested, but he always had something going on. Our friendship was to become the building block of our relationship. But the reality was that things were always kind of lop-sided. I continued believing that the friendship was solid, that people could change for the better, that if I showed love by example, it would be learned and returned, and that if he was willing to work on his relationship with God that everything past friendship would be sustainable. However, I was mistaken.

Here is where I take my onus and accept that I was out of order. When the "committed" relationship began, I attended church probably more out of formality than anything else. It was what you did on Sunday. I would pray to say thanks for life, food, and small victories, but I was not actively reading, seeking, following, listening, or even really hearing His voice. I went to church, heard some good sermons, felt uplifted, and went on with life. On a few occasions, I remember having cried my eyes and heart out to God on Saturday night or even Sunday morning and receiving an on-time word that I knew was just for me! I would always thank Him for the immediate answer but seldom did what I was instructed. I had unknowingly stepped outside of the absolute will of God and went full steam ahead into the permissive. It would be about 15 years before I realized that's what happened.

One day things just weren't ok. I had no inner peace. Everything was in turmoil. The person I thought was my friend, seemed in action and in sight to be more of an enemy. There'd been instances of physical abuse which I covered because love covers right? I was constantly enduring emotional and verbal bashings for unknown reasons other than the fact that he was unhappy with life and wanted to inflict that on me. I could not make sense of anything. I'd lost myself and I had no idea where to begin looking.

New Years' Eve 2017, I opted not to attend Watch Night Service because it was too cold for the baby and planned "family time" at home together. At midnight, I prayed and watched the ball drop with my children. The following Sunday, like clockwork, I got up, got us dressed, and off to church we went. The only thing I can remember of that first week of 2018, is the overwhelming feeling that this can't be life and wondering "How did I end up here?" Honestly, "here" didn't even have specific GPS coordinates. I was knee-deep in post-partum anxiety and couldn't find a clinician. I could only turn to God. I prayed for help and one day while scrolling through Facebook, I came across a challenge called Break the Cycle. It was 5 days of morning and evening teachings with a community of believers and every topic hit home for me. It was everything that I needed! It was my re-introduction to all things Jesus. God answered each and every prayer, cry, and groan of my heart to become whole and get back to Him.

I would love to tell you that life was a cakewalk after that, but it wasn't. The one thing that remained and grew was my faith and knowledge in and of the Lord. Without Him guiding me, I would have drowned in it all, but I am here because He kept me to be able to tell the story. Through the hurt, pain, and monsoons, (forget rain), He guided me. Not because I was so great, but because I began to pray differently. I asked for His will and His will alone to be done. His will had to reign supreme. It became my focal point in every area of my life.

One of the hardest things to come out of agreement with when you're in the wrong is the fact you are actually wrong. We want to defend our thoughts and actions to the end of the end. But for some things there really is no defense. We did what we wanted to do and it went terribly. The end. Even in having landed in this abusive relationship, I had to accept that I walked into it. Dived was probably more like it. I had to make a choice, my will or God's. And it was clear, that what I wanted was complete trash and not working. I had to trade my will for His. So, I did and have not regretted anything since.

TAKHIA GAITHER

LESSON 3
Give Me All the Re's

"Now I am giving him to the Lord, and he will belong to Him his whole life."   *- 1 Samuel 1:28*

Usually, you hear this scripture when someone is "blessing" babies, boys in particular. In other spaces, it's called Christening, but since our kids come to the altar with names already, they're not being Christened. They're being blessed and dedicated. Regardless of what you call it, it's not an uncommon scripture to hear in reading or as a prayer. I know I have prayed it over my sons. I am pretty sure that somewhere in life, my parents, grandparents, and godparents prayed it over me as I have, in fact, belonged to the Lord my whole life. A whole church kid. You know that song "At the Church" by Mark Selvie? I probably could have written it myself. Any of my friends could have. We did everything there. We went to kids' church, sang in the choir, ushered, sat in Bible class (youth and adult), were at the revivals, did homework, made friends, learned to decorate, and this list could keep going. We did it all until we just didn't. And "didn't" looked differently for everyone. For me, I went away to college, I only participated in things when I came home on break if I felt like it. After graduation, I became a mostly Sunday saint, keyword mostly.

I never completely stopped going to church or reading the Bible and definitely always kept my faith. Admittedly, I didn't listen very well, or at all in some cases. The result was a lot of things that I really don't talk about much. They weren't tragic but they were far less than stellar. I just kind of lived, but I was really stuck in a place. Sometimes people can be more descriptive about where they're stuck. I couldn't. To this day, I really can't say where or even why I was stuck. I just was. It was just a place. Lackluster, humdrum, pretty indescribable yet unhappy, stagnant, stale air place. Since I couldn't figure out how to move, I just got comfortable and stayed there. Every time I thought about leaving, I had some idea of why I shouldn't, so I didn't, and I just stayed longer. Each decision to stay was worse than the one before it, but it was like I was in cement and could not move.

2017 was a very difficult year. By February, my oldest son had strep throat twice and the flu, I went to the doctor for what I thought was strep throat, and surprisingly it was the announcement of son #2. The pregnancy and delivery were Emmy award-winning TV show and good Lifetime movie quality events. Had an ankle injury, no rest, a flare-up of an autoimmune condition, totaled a vehicle (thank God we were safe, but it could have been ugly), needed a new place to live, moved 5 seconds before going into labor, fought depression and anxiety and the list could keep going like a ticker tape. By New Year's Eve, I was done. I felt vacant. Looking back at pictures of me, I looked vacant. My eyes had no shine. I was just here. That night, I sat on my living room floor with my boys, playing games and watching Dick Clark. I opted not to go to church because it was extremely cold and I still wasn't well but just like any other NYE, at midnight I prayed. I was thankful to see the year go and optimistic to usher in the new one, but I knew something had to change. I made the decision that night, no more missing church on Sunday, unless I completely had to, and I was going back to studying and reading. That was my first "re-," *recommitment*. I couldn't always attend bible study in person, so I found a few online that I liked to follow and became an immediate fan of the Facebook page, "I Need a Word" and YouVersion Bible plans.

The more I stuck to my commitment, the harder things got. And then, the scales started tipping. I noticed things that previously bothered me, weren't anymore. I could look at the situation and not respond. I wasn't moved by who did or didn't show up for me. I was fine and happy with showing up for myself but even with that, I could not seem to break the cement. In October 2018, I found myself in front of the one place that I hadn't been to in years, the altar. It was Women's Day at Kingdom Nation Church & Ministries, and I was "gifted" a t-shirt with the theme, "I am H.E.R., Healed, Empowered, Restored." When I walked into church that morning, I felt anything but restored, and healing and empowerment weren't even thoughts. By the time I left service that day, I knew the cement was breaking. *Restoration* was coming to me. On New Year's Eve 2018, going into 2019 the sermon was about the 18th year being the end of some things. I wasn't sure what was ending, but I gave God praise in advance for it. I spent a lot of time thinking about that sermon. Although the message was great, I wasn't in year 18 where things were going to break, but I was close. Things were moving, the cement was cracking, and I was *rebuilding* from the inside out.

I honored my recommitment, I held on to my restoration and by April of 2019 I was on to the next "re-," *reclaimed*!! It was beyond clear to me that God called me His own. He *reminded* me that I belonged to Him. As I stood fast and refused to let go, more things came that I had no idea what to do with or how to deal with. Turn after turn, thing after thing, I continued to persevere. Through my perseverance, I found my *resilience*. I love the song "I Didn't Know My Own Strength," by Whitney Houston. On my darkest days, I would put it on repeat, sometimes I'd sing along other times I just let the tears flow until I turned it off. I had lost sight of myself for so long that I'd forgotten how strong I was. Even as I'm writing now, I stop to reflect and take a moment to just thank God for not leaving me. He walked me through everything. Held my hand like a toddler and led me out of the mess that I created because I didn't listen to start with, (long story for another day, but woo child is it a doozy!).

I marched through 2019 with a level of determination that was unparalleled. In the end, the cement that was holding steady now had big cracks in it with a few chips and broken pieces.

2020 was my 18th year! Standing on my recommitment, walking in restoration, continuing my reclamation as God's precious daughter while powering through everything with the resilience He gave me, I began to see things be *released*. I was released from self-inflicted expectations, from toxic relationships, from an assignment that met its end, from the worry and stress of not being able to do what I know He's called me to do, from any high thing that tried to exalt itself above the word of God over my life. I came into 2021 **rededicated**, **renewed**, and **reminded** that I have been His my whole life and will remain His for the rest of my life.

No matter where you are in your walk you too can have all the "re-'s." It starts with a decision. I was dedicated as a baby, baptized at 12, received the Holy Ghost at 14, and restarted everything at 40. It's not too late for you to begin your transformation. Life happens, we don't listen, we miss the warnings, but God allows us to return home. He's not looking for perfection. He wants a heart willing to obey, ears that are ready to hear, and a vessel that's willing to do. I'm sure that my list of "re-'s" is far from over and they may be different from yours, but here is a journal topic for you. I'm going to give you a list of 10 Re-'s. Take some time to think about what each of them means to you and write it down. Are you ready?? Here we go!

1. Recommitted
2. Restored
3. Reclaimed
4. Resilient
5. Released
6. Renewed
7. Rededicated
8. Reminded

9. Redefined
10. Reintroduced

Is transformation easy?? No, it's not but you don't have to do it alone. I started alone in my living room having a me and God moment, (the boys were asleep by 11:45 pm!). The more I honored the commitment and became intentional about it, He sent the community and the people I needed to remain on the path. No, it is not easy, but it is completely worth it. Make the choice to obey God, take one step, He's got you for the rest of them.

TAKHIA GAITHER

LESSON 4
The Wise Words of Mommy

"...Don't neglect your mother's instruction. What you learn from them will crown you with grace and be a chain of honor around your neck"   *- Proverbs 1:8-9*

The relationship between a mother and her son(s) is unparalleled and indescribable. They hold your heart, cause you concern, make you smile, and at times in 2020, make you wish you could keep them in a bubble to protect them. We want to shield our sons from everything so that they are not swallowed by the cruelty of this world. Yet, we have the charge to instruct them, guide them, and leave the rest to God.

This is an open letter to my boys and to any boys, (big or small), who may be missing the instructions of their mother. May you one day read it and let these lessons become a crown of grace and a chain of honor around your neck.

Lesson 1: God first.

If you remember nothing else, this first lesson covers everything. Take the time to seek God for yourself and seek His instructions about everything. Prayer is not just something you do on Sunday in church, or over your food, or when something bad happens. It's ongoing and often. It is your two-way conversation with God. It's not only about you talking to Him; once you speak your heart, learn to be still, and wait for Him to talk back to you. It is especially important that you establish your own relationship with God. Learn all that you can about Him and how He thinks of you. Always remember, you are His son before mine—I just have you on loan. He is an awesome Father. He guides your mother—allow Him to guide you. Don't let the brevity of this paragraph fool you. The actual lesson packs a punch far greater than can be written here. In fact, I could also stop here, but there is much more for me to tell you.

Lesson 2: Control your emotions; don't allow them to control you.

Life is full of all kinds of things and a range of emotions. You will be excited, happy, mad, sad, upset, and worried. And it is okay to be all those things. Allow yourself to feel what you feel but take the time to learn how to do so in ways that are not destructive to you or to others. As you grow, do not allow your negative emotions to overtake you to the point that others see you as irrational and confrontational. Please understand, in the times we live in, because you are a young, Black man, this is how you are seen without ever opening your mouth.

Do not give anyone the satisfaction of fitting you into a negative stereotype. Keep Proverbs 15:1-2 at the forefront of your thoughts: "A gentle answer deflects anger, but harsh words make tempers flare. The tongue of the wise makes knowledge appealing but the mouth of a fool belches out foolishness."

Self-control is a fruit of the spirit that gets overlooked often because when people are upset, they use that as an excuse to not be in control of the things they say and the actions in which they choose to participate. It can be hard not to react using your first thought, and it takes some time to learn how to do this, but in the times when you can't see how to or even know where to begin, go back to Lesson 1! Pray and ask God for His peace, for His calm, and for His direction and guidance in the situation. As you grow, pay remarkably close attention to the examples you have before you. Find the ones who exhibit self-control and decide to learn from them. Ask questions and have conversations that will lead you to learn how to self-regulate.

Lesson 3: Be accountable.

When unfavorable things happen, it is extremely easy to blame someone or something else for the situation at hand. Before paying attention to the finger that is pointed at someone or something else, take a moment to look again at the three pointing back at you. This is not a request or permission to take the blame for things that do not belong to you. This **IS** a call to action to evaluate your own part in the situation. Was there anything in your actions that could have contributed to this result? As Bugs Bunny used to say in cartoons, was there a place where you "probably should have taken a left at Albuquerque?" Could you have used a different tone? Did you act out of love? Do not beat yourself up or pour over details but do reflect on the entire situation instead of the parts. Be willing and able to take responsibility for your actions in any and every situation.

There will be times that even after you've thought and re-thought about things you will still have no idea what just happened or why there's smoke. When this happens, (I say when because it will), go back to Lesson 1. Pray for direction and guidance. There is an old saying: "Don't ask God why." Or perhaps you've heard, "You don't question God." I think that it's a matter of what you're asking. You don't question God's will and what He allows or what He uses. But it's a natural response to wonder, "God, why is this happening?" What happens next is the reason I believe that old saying came about.

In asking God why (or any other question), you must be willing to receive the answer and the correction that may come with it. If there is an incident that appears out of the blue, but God reveals that it happened because of something that happened a while before, the correct action is to take responsibility for your role and seek further direction. There are many at this phase who will not accept the correction and go back to blame. With the questions come answers, and because He is the good father that He is, all the answers won't be what you want to hear, but they will be the answers nonetheless. The only person you have control over in any situation is YOU. You control your actions; you control the things you say. Being accountable keeps you in a posture to continually seek God to help you because what you know has limits. What He knows is limitless!

Lesson 4: Everybody can't go.

This goes with Lesson 3. People are in your life for reasons, seasons, or lifetimes. When you try to hold on to those who were only meant to be there for a specific reason or during a specific time, you impede your growth. This is not about a cut-off game. It is knowing and recognizing that sometimes we outgrow people or that people outgrow us and it's all perfectly okay. It doesn't make them bad people and things don't have to end horribly. In life, your goal should always be to grow in every way: spiritually, personally, and professionally. Growth is important. A part of that is understanding that everybody can't go.

As much as you would love to take certain people with you on the journey, they may not be able to handle your next level. It can be hard to let go of relationships, especially when you genuinely care for and about people, but it is also necessary to understand that your growth may not include them. Back to Lesson 1—pray for God to heighten your discernment so that you will be able to understand the places and spaces that are being prepared for you and who is in them. Invoke Lesson 2. If someone shows that they are not willing to be a part of your next season, or you just begin to feel the pull of God in another direction, you can still greet and see them with love, but set boundaries for you and for them. This carries into Lesson 3. The boundaries are to hold you accountable to yourself and understand when you get close to exceeding a limit.

Relationships have lasting effects on us, good and bad. Sometimes we don't see the bad until we're out of it and growing. Remain prayerful and true to who God has made you to be and decide to grow anyway, even if it means that you'll walk alone. (Lesson 4a - You're NEVER alone. He's always with you and will always send you exactly who you need).

Lesson 5: Read the Bible for yourself.

There are people who will pick and choose what they decide you should know about the Word of God. Be careful of people who always have a verse to point out what you are doing wrong, but never seem to know or use those same ones to address their own actions, or who only know Scripture to support their actions. Read, pray, ask for, and get an understanding of your own. Studying for yourself builds your relationship with God. I can lead you to Him. I can tell you about Him. I can teach you all the things, but at the end of the day, you are responsible for your learning, (Low-key that's lesson #6; as a teacher, I can go on about that for days).

Taking responsibility goes back to Lesson 3. Reading the Word for yourself will help you learn what being accountable for yourself looks like. What are the things that God counts as righteousness? What are the things that you need to do to always show Him on the earth? Yes, paying attention in church is a start, but learning happens on more than Sunday mornings or during weekly Bible study. It's an ongoing, never-ending process. Write the word "on the tablet of your heart" (Proverbs 3:3, NIV).

In closing ...

It is my charge to train you up in the way that you should go so that as you get older, you will not depart from it (Proverbs 22:6, paraphrased). I know that you will be great men of God. To see you in action amazes me daily. You are brilliant, you are important, your life matters, you matter, you are loved. One day when you're older, it is my prayer that you will think about these lessons and the countless others and that they will have become not only life lessons but life habits that you are now teaching to your own children and to those who will have the pleasure of coming in contact with you. I love you always.

Mommy

LESSON 5
Stop Being Vomit

"As a dog returns to its vomit, so a fool repeats his foolishness."   *- Proverbs 26:11*

You've seen the title, read the scripture, and now your mind is probably racing and wondering about a few things. Am I right? It's cool. I got you. So let me clear them up for you before we go any further. I am not calling anyone literal vomit, a dog, or a fool (well, that last one, might happen, IJS, pray for me). Jesus taught in parables and analogies. As a teacher, He's my number one role model, so I tend to lean toward that especially when it involves matters of the heart. I need this to stay with you. Get your pencils/pens, something to take some notes on, maybe some tissues, and let's get to work.

Many of us have had, or may even be currently in, the unpleasant experience of what appears to be the never-ending relationship. You know the ones I'm talking about. Fall out, break up, get back together, fall out again, break up again, get back together … again. This cycle just keeps turning and just like John Legend's song, it becomes "Another Again." (That used to be one of my favorite songs, smh at myself.) Anyhow, this is a no-judgment zone. I'm not telling you anything I have not lived through myself. I had one of those relationships. It lasted for a very long time. In case no one else has informed you, these relationships are incredibly unhealthy. Mentally, spiritually, emotionally, physically – just completely unhealthy. In part, I personally blame '90s and early 2000s R&B; it messed us up. I love Mary J. Blige, (MJB), but "Be Without You" is the biggest mind-trap of a song. For real, go check the lyrics. We loved it because parts of it are true—you should want a relationship full of truth, honesty, and loyalty and if you're giving that out you want it back. But there is one part that I realized was the end of the rope for me. In paraphrasing, she says she'll be up until he comes back home because she can't sleep without him. Insert side-eye, neck roll, eye roll, Rick Roll, all of it! Well maybe exclude Rick because this is definitely a thing that you should give up and have no remorse about letting down.

The problem with toxic relationships is that we think things like staying and waiting show our love, loyalty, and care while proving to the other person that we are it. We are "the one." They should love us because we check all the boxes. Sadly, it does not prove any of that at all. It proves that we need to create and enforce some serious boundaries. Take it from lived experience. If that joker has repeatedly left and come back, the next time he leaves, bolt your door, pray for his soul, go to sleep, and let him stay gone. As long as he or she can come in and out like a revolving door, they will.

This is where our opening scripture and the title come into play. If you're squeamish, I apologize in advance. Think about vomit for a minute. List out all the things you know about it. It's disgusting, the only part of it that may dissolve is whatever part is water. The rest of it stays in the form that it is when it comes out. It is proof and evidence that your body is rejecting something. Let that last part sit with you for a moment. It is the thing your body rejects. In these relationships, we become vomit. We are not disgusting literally; disgust becomes an overwhelming feeling as we are the thing that is constantly rejected and left in whatever form we are in when it all comes apart. Whatever dissolves of what we are feeling leaves through the tears we cry from sadness, anger, or possibly some combination. We remain there in a puddle to get washed away, turned to dust, (have you ever seen that stuff that school janitors use), or just left there to be walked around and walked over. Today, I want you to stop being vomit.

Have you ever watched a dog return to his vomit? He spits it up and out then runs off to go do whatever else he wants to do and then sometime later, decides to circle back to it. When he gets back to it, he sniffs it and then licks it back up like nothing ever happened. I can't say if he really gets all of it up. I really don't feel like he does. There are still remnants and pieces left on the ground as they were.

Now let's bring this back to us. They leave us, go do whatever they want at times with whoever else they want, and then come back to scoop us up like they're doing us a favor. They return expecting open arms from us, and because we love them, we go along with it. Sometimes it's a cross between love and being parents or we've been together going strong for way too long because we're still holding on to MJB – relationships go through things, this is just another thing, what we have is real. We'll come out of it and build stronger and better. We're happy to have been discarded because it somehow means our relationship will now and forever be Ford-tough. And it is until it happens again. Just writing about it makes me exhausted. I have no idea how I managed to live this cycle for so long. On second thought, I do. God saved me from me because the relationship was sent to be my destruction. I implore you, please stop being vomit.

I hear you thinking. "Takhia, I want to stop being vomit, but I don't know how to. I don't know where to start or what to do. To be honest, I don't even know if I really want to stop." I get it. These were my same thoughts. It hurt to stay, and it equally hurt to even think of letting go, much less actually doing it. But I want you to take a moment and make a list. Draw a line down the middle of a piece of paper. On one side, write out the positives of your relationship. On the other side, write out the negatives. No holds barred, but here's the challenge. Be honest with yourself. For me, I really had to sit with this for a while.

Quick story: the thing that made me do this very exercise was a Facebook memory. The picture was of a smiling couple who had a great time on a family vacation. We returned home early in the morning because of some commitments, still happy. By noon, all the happiness was gone just because I asked what we were doing that evening. The result: he left, went on a date, (yes you read that correctly), slept with her, and then came back the next morning and got mad at me for being upset that he did wrong. Realistically, that should have been the end, but sadly it was not. Fast forward, some years later, I saw the picture, smiled slightly, then suddenly my demeanor switched. The part of the memory not captured by the photo was that right after we took the picture, I stepped away to the restroom. When I returned, he was already on the phone lining up the date for when we got back.

What I started to realize as I looked through photo after photo was that each of them had these dual memories. There were very few events if any, to be honest, that did not. Each one was surrounded by some unfavorable event. I sat down, made my list, and decided that day. The decision to stop being vomit begins with you deciding to take off the rose-colored glasses. I had to stop making excuses for what was happening and look at what was happening. As you make your list, I need you to do the same thing. Every relationship has highs and lows. We're human, we won't agree all the time. But to tap into the B-clause of our scripture, there should be far more good memories than foolishness. Being vomit is in fact foolish. Remaining in the relationship is foolish.

There are things that you can't always go around, go over, or go under. Sometimes the way out is through. The decision to stop being vomit is one of the ones you must walk through. It starts with a choice. You must become sick and tired of being sick and tired. One of the many things I had to come to grips with was that each time I was praying to save the relationship, God was really showing me the way out. If this has resonated with you, He has shown you as well. In Jeremiah 29:11 we learn His plans for us are never for harm, they are always for our good. These types of relationships are harm and not God. You can break the cycle. Make the choice to be God's best and not man's vomit.

TAKHIA GAITHER

LESSON 6
Faking the Function

"Having therefore obtained the help of God, I continue unto this day, witnessing to both small and great ..."
- Acts 26:22 (KJV)

Functional depression. Two words that aren't often used together, yet it is probably more common than anyone realizes. No, it's not a DSM-5 diagnosis but it does affect many high-functioning people. I was a functional depressant for years but didn't really know until years later. As I was going through it, all I knew was that I wasn't entirely okay and it seemed like the more I reached for help, the more help evaded me.

I spent most of 2017 pregnant. When it was close to my due date, I received the obligatory talk about postpartum depression and how if I wasn't feeling much like myself some of that was normal but if I felt like I was going to do harm to myself or to the baby please call someone immediately. That conversation was understandably necessary, but it wasn't very comforting. The problem was that I was already not feeling like myself. My entire pregnancy was nothing short of a bad *Lifetime* movie from the 80s, (I've watched a few recently and they seem to have gotten better). It was more than depression. There was a level of sheer panic that came over me. I was so wound up that years later I am wondering if my mental state played a severe role in being pre-eclamptic. I'll be researching that soon, but I digress. Mothers like to go into the birthing phase having some level of assurance regarding their household affairs, employment, care for other children, space, and preparations in place for the new one coming. It's joyous and anxious at the same time but there should definitely be more joy than angst, right?

Yet in the middle of not feeling myself, I still had to teach. I still had to mother. I still had to function. But oddly, and equally sadly, this wasn't anything new. My answer to not feeling like myself had always been to dive into some project, job, school, or something. It didn't really matter what it was, so long as my mind was occupied, and I didn't have to deal with whatever was bothering me. Growing up in church I always heard, "An idle mind is the devil's workshop." I wasn't interested in being possessed or the devil having anything to do with me or my mind, so I was sure to keep busy. One time in college, I had 3 jobs, was in school, and was on the regional board for a national organization. In my world, I didn't have time to be depressed, I was too busy. However, being pregnant, already a mother, working full time, and having an autoimmune condition to keep under wraps, this was clearly not the time to take on a new task. I can't lie, as I sat in the hospital, I actually contemplated finding something.

Delivery was a *Grey's Anatomy* emergency room scene complete with all the people yelling and screaming and me being sedated. When I woke up, my little guy was here and in perfect health. Seeing him subsided some of whatever I had going on but even after delivery, I was still not okay. I had panic attacks for almost a week because I could not lie down without feeling like I couldn't breathe. Months after he was born, I remember standing in my kitchen and explaining to his father that I was experiencing postpartum depression. He appeared concerned and sympathetic, but it was short-lived. In hindsight, a large part of what set this spin in motion was that relationship. I began to feel trapped. It was overwhelming and I was right on the brink of believing the biggest lie that the enemy tells anyone, "You are alone."

This was not my first round of depression, but it was by far the absolute worst. By 2017, I'd prayed my way through depression at least 2 other times, probably more. This is not a badge of honor. The reality is that I probably should have sought help sooner. Of those times, one was a side effect of a medication, and the others were situational. The answers seemed and were pretty simple: stop taking the medicine and do things so that the situation would improve so that my mood would improve, which usually involved some sort of cut-off game. This was different. I couldn't shake it. I had no help at home. I had to function at work. I could not break down. I tried contacting clinicians and was told that since I wasn't suicidal or going to harm the baby or anyone else, I should try to rest, relax, and do things that I enjoyed to improve my mood and limit stress. Limit stress … right. New baby, a kindergartner, seemingly always a house full of people that weren't always helpful, and a partner who seemed more like an acquaintance, not to mention, experiencing a flare-up of my autoimmune condition, recovering from a c-section, and preparing to go back to work because if I stayed out any longer, I wouldn't get paid. Limit stress, got it, smooth on it.

I want to be clear. Just because I took this walk alone, does not mean that you should. I went alone until I could find a counselor that was a good fit. If you have not already done so, please seek the help of a medical professional. If you're not sure where to start, speak to a general practitioner or your primary care physician if you have one. They will be able to direct you to services and counselors. If you're not ready to go the medical route, seek out the help of a coach. Understand that coaches are amazing resources, but they are not therapists. They cannot diagnose you or prescribe medication, but they can provide you with activities and information to help you begin to work through what you're feeling and dealing with. Also, during this time, build what I like to call your "circle of safety". Your circle of safety may be family members, close friends, or even a support group where you can have true and honest conversations without judgment. These are the people who are in place to support and encourage you. They are your "amen" corner. They rejoice with you on great days, and they cry with you on not-so-great days. They are your support. Understand that, unlike coaches and counselors, more times than not your family and friends are not trained professionals. While they are there for love, support, and care, they may not give the best advice or be able to give you any for processing through this.

I understand that it is hard to trust anyone with the chaos in your head. I completely get it. While I was a functional depressant, I was also in denial for a very long time. I'd managed to convince myself that I was fine and that it would blow over, I just needed to add another activity and things would be okay. Although I was never suicidal, I was very close to the path to insanity. I know reading all of this, it's very easy to think and feel that it's all good to know but you don't think you can do it or that it's not going to work for you. I'm here to tell you that you can do this. Picking up this book was just the start. As you read, think, and even take notes, allow yourself to write out what you're feeling, and allow God to talk to you as you read and reflect. Give yourself grace and patience. It may take some time to find help. Don't lose heart. God hears; He knows, He sees, and He cares.

Having obtained no help from any outside source, (the complete opposite of Acts 26:22), I turned to the one place that I knew had never failed me and would always help me. With a level of determination that superseded any that I'd ever used for any reason, I ran after God. I had no choice. I was at rock bottom. I had nothing left. I was a shell of myself. I began to read, pray and study almost all day every day. The YouVersion Bible app became my best friend. When I couldn't read physically, I would turn on the audio version in the car, in the house while I was cooking, at my desk at work, or standing in line at the store. Some people create affirmation walls and cards to encourage themselves. In my desk drawer, I had a ring of index cards that I would write scriptures on one side and a brief reflection on the back. On one of my file cabinet drawers, I had post-it notes with scriptures on them that would encourage me throughout the day. Here are 7 of my favorites:

1. *Exodus 14:13-14: But Moses told the people, "Don't be afraid. Just stand still and watch the Lord rescue you today. The Egyptians you see today will never be seen again. The Lord himself will fight for you. Just stay calm."*

   Whatever you face today, you will not face tomorrow because God fights for you always. You don't have to be anxious. You don't have to fear. You can stay calm, He's got you.

2. *John 16:33: I have told you all this so that you may have peace in me. Here on earth, you will have many trials and sorrows. But take heart because I have overcome the world.*

   When Jesus hung and died on the cross, He took on everything that we will ever feel and deal with. He went to hell, fought, and defeated them all for us. Since He has overcome the world, we can overcome anything.

3. *Amos 9:13: "The time will come," says the Lord, "when the grain and grapes will grow faster than they can be harvested."*

Do yourself a favor and read this one in The Message version. It starts off saying, "It won't be long now." Everything has an ending, there is a time and a season for it all, and today's sorrow has an end. There will come a day when things move so fast in your favor that God will blow your mind.

4. *Jude 24: Now all glory to God, who is able to keep you from falling away and will bring you with great joy into his glorious presence without a single fault.* This is my "hallelujah anyhow" verse. Despite how you feel, find a Thank You Jesus, a Lord, I love You, a God, You are awesome. It may not change the actual situation, but praise is an immediate mood enhancer. It takes your focus off your concern or situation and places it on God. Once He has your focus, the outcome is limitless.

5. *Psalms 23:2-4: He lets me rest in green meadows; he leads me beside peaceful streams. He renews my strength. He guides me along the right paths, bringing honor to his name. Even when I walk through the darkest valley, I will not be afraid, for you are close beside me. Your rod and your staff protect and comfort me.*

We can walk and live in peace because He is with us. We do not have to wrestle with the torment. He is always near no matter where we go, no matter what we face. He always protects and comforts us.

6. *Philippians 4:8: Finally, brothers and sisters, whatever is true, whatever is noble, whatever is right, whatever is pure, whatever is lovely, whatever is admirable—if anything is excellent or praiseworthy—think about such things.*

When our minds begin to wander to things that are not going well, not pleasant, and often frustrating, it is at those moments we should stop and reset our thinking on things that are good and pleasing: the laughter or smile of a close friend, a good time we have had at an event, the faithfulness of God — meditate on the times He has shown up in your life. Even if there is nothing that we can personally find, turn your thoughts to those of the Father. Admire the beauty of a garden or artwork. Find your favorite praise and worship song and dwell in the goodness of the Lord.

7. *Matthew 21:22: If you believe, you will receive whatever you ask for in prayer.*

The road to recovery is just a short prayer away. Pray for God's guidance in selecting a counselor or a physician and pray for the renewing of your mind and your heart. Pray for your healing. In all things pray for His will to be performed in your life. After you have prayed, activate your faith, and believe. Walk in the victory that you know is coming.

I could keep doing this all day. What was supposed to be my motivation drawer, turned into a motivation wall, and before long, I found myself not needing to see the wall, I would just recall them at the appropriate time. It was the first time in a long time that I actually knew what it meant to hide the word in your heart.

I would love to tell you that I don't have a struggle from time to time or that I never had to deal with depression again. The truth is, sometimes I find myself going back into the place of "I need to do something else." It's my comfort zone and it became my crutch. The difference between me then and me now is, is that at this point, I now know when I am entering that mode and I'm no longer scared to do the work or have the conversation with my coach, counselor, or circle of safety to begin to self-regulate. Recovery was and is a partnership between me and God. I rely on, trust, and believe Him to be a healer and a mind regulator. He trusts me with His instructions. Having obtained help from the Lord, I continue to this day, and I am a living witness that if He did it for me, He can and will do it for you.

TAKHIA GAITHER

LESSON 7
Always a Work in Progress

Ephesians 4:2 says "Always be humble and gentle. Be patient with each other making allowance for each other's faults because of your love." And even as I put the closing period and quotation marks comes the huge sigh and if I'm honest, a slight eye roll. This is one of those scriptures that personally pricks my heart, but I also know that while it's pricking, it's healing, and I have to let it work.

Being completely transparent, people really have a way of getting on ALL my nerves. Like "no troll left behind," I really feel like they are King Poppy Troll but instead of screaming "No troll left behind," they are screaming "No nerve left behind!!!" (If you've never seen Trolls, I suggest giving it a look; a cute movie with so many messages but I digress...). I really do try to always keep the fruit of the spirit in the forefront of my mind, so that I constantly allow the Holy Spirit to check me when my fruit's not showing. But then, there is that time that comes when I've exceeded every limit of everything and in those moments, I'm not worried about being humble or patient and we're not even going to bring up love. In my younger years, if your actions took me to that point, I let you have it. No holds barred. No words barred and most of them were probably, (more like definitely), ungodly. Not one shred of care for the feelings, emotions, or intentions of the other person. Now because the Holy Spirit is the ultimate checker, I would always repent for being out of order and ungodly and on some occasions, I would apologize to the individual that was the recipient of my rage. In my 40s, I have learned that when I feel those things starting to rise, I immediately stop and pray first. Doing that allows me to calm down and be able to react accordingly. It took some work to get to that point.

This scripture was the verse of the day at a time when I was going through a really difficult situation. I had not exploded, nor was I really planning to, but somewhere in my train of thought, I couldn't pinpoint how loving I'd be able to be either. In reading Ephesians 4:2 the first thing I said was, "Ok Jesus, I hear You. But I don't know how. I am hurt. I am upset. I'm angry, frustrated, and I'm really not trying to be any of those things. I don't know what to do or how to do it." The answer I got back was a simple question, "Takhia, where is your heart?" And then everything made sense to me.

The existence of the rage and negative feelings was because my heart is, and has been, in a place to do for others; to show love and care for others. It was one of the main drivers in the path of my career. Teaching public school had to have a greater reason than a paycheck. If I didn't love my kids and love what I did, their learning wasn't going to happen. I had to get back to my why, not just for teaching but for life in general.

Why do I show honor to a person who has seemingly dishonored me? Why do I continue to give love and care to people who have clearly done things that are unlovable? Why do I bother continuing to try? The answer is the posture of my heart. I used to call it a gift and a curse, but then I realized things from God are never cursed, that was a false belief provided by the enemy to derail me from walking in my true potential and purpose.

Society calls us empaths. We feel everybody's pain. We want to help. We take on too much. AND, rarely, if ever ask for anything in return, but we would like for someone to do those same things for us should we ever need them. Our hearts are in good places. We are trying to show love, care, and compassion, just like Jesus did. Or I'll speak for myself, that's what I thought I was doing. What produced the rage was when despite having shown all the love and care in the world, I repeatedly did not get that back from the individual or overall situation. At today years old, I have come to grips with   2   things:

1. Forgiveness does not require access.
2. I'll always be a work in progress.

See, the point of my frustrations has been that while I've shown forgiveness, because my heart was to help, at some point, I should have ceased access. In my flawed thinking, I equated cutting them off and not loving them through whatever was going on, with not showing love and forgiveness. I'd missed a very important part of showing love to others. I did well with love thy neighbor from the 10 Commandments standpoint. But I was doing horribly at loving myself. Mark 12:30-31 clearly outlines the conditions/levels/steps, whatever word you would like to use for them, to fulfill the greatest commandment.

Far too often, especially as women, we find ourselves on the short end of the stick with one of them because we're expected to be everything to everyone except for ourselves. We are good for "loving the Lord with all of our heart, soul, mind, and strength," (Mark 12:30). The part where many of us, myself included, fail miserably is verse 31, "Love your neighbor as YOU LOVE YOURSELF." For most of my adult life, there has not been a push for anyone to love themselves, mostly due to flawed theology that led people to believe, preach and teach, that loving yourself was a complete sin and that all of your focus should be on showing love to others, (my loose interpretation and summation of 2 Timothy 3:2 and other scriptures that mention the perils of vanity). Within the last 10 years or so, there has been more talk about loving yourself first but for that to be effective we must realize that there is, in fact, a difference between *being a lover of yourself* and *having love for yourself.* Too many times these things are taken to be synonymous and they are not.

To have self-love is to care for yourself. It is to be concerned with your well-being and your spiritual, emotional, physical, psychological, and financial health. It is understanding what makes you tick and being able to do things that grow and nurture you. Loving yourself is being able to sit and spend time with yourself and just let it be a "you and God moment." When you accomplish something, you don't have to boast or brag but do be proud of yourself and "big-up" yourself.

To be a lover of yourself is to place yourself in a headspace where you can do no wrong and everything you do is grand. The problems that you face are not due to any shortcomings of your own, but they are strictly due to everybody else having a problem with themselves. In loving yourself you are able to take accountability and responsibility for yourself and your actions. When you are a lover of self those things are absent. Everything you do is always the by-product of what someone else has done, real or perceived. Not overwhelmingly enlightening, but if you need permission from this point forward to healthily love yourself, you have it. Mark 12:31 gives it to you.

Now let's put Mark 12:31 into the context of what Ephesians 4:2 is instructing, do the work and begin to let the healing begin. If I am loving myself, would I yell, scream, and holler at myself? Would I belittle myself? Would I lie to myself? Would I steal from myself? Would I be uncaring or unkind to myself? My answers to these questions will always be a resounding no! So, then why would I continue to allow people who did these things to me to have access to me? None of those things are associated with love. This was the eureka moment!!

The resolution, simple in words but not always so much indeed, let them go! Forgive and forget is actually a colloquialism that is also interpreted poorly. Forget does not mean to completely disregard that it happened. It means if you intend to forgive, you cannot constantly bring it to the remembrance of the person who offended you, especially if they are earnestly and sincerely trying to make amends for poor behavior. In my poor interpretation, I took it to mean forget the actions AND the way they made me feel. So, I completely canceled the whole thing like it never happened. Let it all go. But then months later, I would find myself sitting in the same situation again because in extending forgiveness I should have said we need to part ways now. What I realized is that the reason why I was so hurt to the point of rage and unable to remain humble, gentle, and act in love was because access to the wounded area should have been denied. I can see your head shaking in agreement, disbelief, or both. And it's ok. We've all done it. The first step to overcoming anything is admitting that there is in fact something to overcome.

This is what lead me to fact #2. I will always be a work in progress. Some people don't like that feeling or knowing that about themselves. As an admitted lifelong learner, it was easy for me to be ok with being in progress because in more than ways one, I'm always in progress with something. I'm making progress towards earning a doctorate. I'm making progress toward becoming a better entrepreneur. I'm progressing at being a better mother. You never have to be completely polished all the time. I will tell you, coming out of agreement with the hurt that's had access to you is not pretty or rosy or a skip in the park. It requires intentionality and commitment and a circle of safety. My circle knows regardless of how together I appear to anyone else, there's tape in the back holding it together. My circle of safety says you don't have to front here. It's ok to not be ok.

I had to sit with the fact that my pursuit of wholeness is a consistent work in progress. I also had to sit with the fact that there are certain life decisions that I made from a place of false wholeness. You know that place, where you think you're good because you've taken *THE* class, had the appropriate numbers of cries, you could clearly see God's hand moving, and it felt like the top of the world? Yep, that place right there! Not realizing that I was still in progress, I made a life-altering decision. There is no other way to describe it than to say, what the enemy meant for evil God has surely and is still working it out for my good.

Although I started writing this with a sigh, I am ending with a smile that I know only comes from God's great joy in my heart. See the key to Ephesians 4:2 is to realize that I can be humble, gentle, patient, and give grace to others through their faults because God gives me grace and showers me with love through my own. And so maybe in my situation, love is having a difficult conversation, all the while knowing that there is a way to approach it and show the love of God. The thing with progress is that you're always supposed to move towards a result. Ceasing access to things you know have hindered your progress is a necessary step. It's ok to be in progress.

LESSON 8
A New Story

"... All these things are gone forever. And the one sitting on the throne said, "Look, I am making everything new!" And then he said to me, "Write this down, for what I tell you is trustworthy and true."   *- Revelation 21:4-5*

Today I declare to anyone reading this, nothing that has happened to you will be your story anymore. Everything changes for you from today forward. The thing that had you bound is broken in the name of Jesus. Seal this moment with praise. If you are not sure what that looks like, lift your hands now and say, "Lord, I thank You and I receive it. It is so in Jesus' name. Amen"

Prayers are usually reserved for the end of chapters and sections, but God said to start with them. As The Ready Write-Her, I write what He says. The enemy tries to convince you "this" will always be your story. No relationship will ever be any different. You will never be any different. Today, we are no longer accepting his lie as truth. God says this will not be our story anymore. It will be the testimony that comes forth as He takes the ashes we've had and gives us the beauty of a new life in Him.

Not many years ago, I stood in the mirror looking at the shell of a woman I'd become and made a similar if not nearly verbatim declaration over myself. I have a story similar to many, but you may rarely hear them spoken. When we tried before, we were told things such as, "You should have known better or prayed on it," or insert any other churchy "rebuke" that comes across more like an "I told you so" than any sort of care or concern. You know the lines.

I grew up in church. I had both parents in the home. I could be trusted to make pretty good decisions. I not only went to church, but I listened and tried to live it out more times than not. So how did I end up fighting for my life in an abusive relationship? Didn't I see the signs? Couldn't I discern it? Did I want a man that bad? There are answers to each of these, some complex, and others a simple yes and no. I can answer the last one for you now. No, I did not want a man so bad that I would endure abuse to keep one.

How Did I Get Here ...

When I began to retrace my steps, I sat thinking about the question of how I got to this place for a while. It didn't make any sense, but at the same time, it did. When it came to learning scriptures and anything about the Bible, I was a very good student. I knew/know a lot. I could recall a lot of scriptures and apply them correctly. I would ask questions. I wanted to know more and understand more because, "in all thy getting, get understanding," (Proverbs 4:7).

Despite that, there was one verse I didn't understand well enough, 2 Corinthians 6:14, "Do not be unequally yoked with unbelievers." It was partly from my own belief, partly from lack of a clear discussion, and partly from being shielded from examples. When you've grown up in church, you see and hear a lot. When you're a child, meaning anyone under 18, sometimes you don't get a lot of answers to things. You see friends who are dating boys who don't go to church. They are told not to be unequally yoked. But you also see friends dating boys in church and no one says don't be unequally yoked to them. They just say stop being fast. The reality though is that some of those church couples were unequally yoked as well.

My poor interpretation led me to date and deal with men who were unequally yoked with me. In my naivety, I figured if he was willing to go to church and listen, then we were good. We could have conversations about God and do life together. Very rarely did that happen, and when it did things were weird, for lack of a better way to write it. The conversations were either so far to the left that I couldn't make sense of them or so far in the other direction it left me frustrated trying to explain. There was no "joy of loving Jesus" conversation. I was either always defending what I believed or always having to overly explain what I believed. Long story short, part of my path to getting to that place was my own faulty understanding.

I Saw the Signs ...

There was a 90's group called Ace of Base and they had a popular song called "The Sign," about a complicated relationship. The song itself is kind of cryptic, but the hook is the part that most people remember. It makes you wonder what signs she saw to open her eyes and make the decision to end the relationship and move on, (later in the song she says she's happy without him and living life). Random sidebar about me, I listened to a lot of music -- gospel and secular, I can probably find a song to fit almost any situation. In dealing with my situation, I turned to music a lot because certain lyrics spoke the things that I had no words for.

I saw signs that said things were unusual. Given the stories I was told, I gave them the benefit of the doubt to be true. Some of them actually were. Others were so far fabricated that if you dug deep enough, you could possibly find the shred of truth that it came from but not always. A few of the red flags were blaring but thanks to various R&B songs from the late 90s to early 2000s, I was convinced that if your "love story" didn't have some kind of drama in it, it wasn't real. I accepted my story as building the drama for the love of my life. Sign after sign came to me like pop flies in centerfield. In a throwback to my days as a centerfielder, one day I misjudged what should have been an easy catch and got hit square in my mouth, knocking a tooth out of the socket, and causing me to bite through my bottom lip. That is exactly what happened to me with all the signs. I misjudged my mark and got hit dead in my face, figuratively and literally. That hit is what really started the next answer.

Discernment in Question …

The thing that people don't realize about discernment is that in order for you to use it effectively, you have to know it exists, #1. You also have to have the ear to actually hear and the eye to actually see, #2. These are not things that happen when your salvation is surface level. You might have a knowing feeling here and there, sometimes you listen, sometimes you don't. Being a woman, we chalk up many things to "woman's intuition" and continue moving along with our day. When we listen, we're pumped saying, "See I knew …" On the other side, when we don't listen, there's the lament, "Why didn't I just listen to my gut?"

In full transparency, had I been reading, studying, and praying on a more consistent basis, I probably could have discerned what was going on. Throughout the relationship, there were a multitude of things occurring that played a part in my lack of discernment. Aside from majoring in Sunday Sainthood, I was also undergoing some health challenges that took a lot of my focus away from anything other than my health. Add to that trying to successfully "be" in my relationship - there were days when I got tired of hearing or listening to anything period, and I definitely wasn't seeing anything. In fact, my health condition caused double vision and other eye problems where it was literally difficult to see clearly.

The punch heard around the world cleared that up, (not really the entire world, but it was heard LOUDLY in my world). It didn't change my health; it's an autoimmune illness that comes and goes. Nearly 1 month before that event, I decided I was going to get back to reading, studying, and praying on a consistent basis because whatever "this" was, it was not my life. It shouldn't have been "life" for anybody, especially and definitely not me. It was close to New Year's, and I decided that January 1 was my new start no matter what happened. I was not going to shake or move from my decision. And I didn't.

The Man I Needed ...

After choosing to rebuild my relationship with God, I didn't immediately exit that relationship. For every temptation, there's a way of escape (1 Corinthians 10:13), but you must be willing to take the escape. I had quite a few chances to escape and only partially took them. I said, "I was checked out," and I was a little. I said, "I was done," and I was a little. I said, "We were done," and I meant it when I said it. Somehow, I would always find myself back on this wheel. It was the worst cycle. You've probably seen a variation of this while in love. It looks like hate, and somebody says, "I'm sorry." You have a heart-to-heart with pledges and promises of them doing better, only to end up back in love again. Yay! Nooo!! There should have never been a yay.

This time, I knew something had to give and be different. I was preparing my exit and a way to break free of all of this, and then disaster struck. There were a series of events that took place that were initially daunting and very draining. I was on the fence about the disaster being the source of my escape. I was close to taking it and then it happened. What is it you ask? The grand epiphany. The statement of love and adoration I had been waiting to hear for years, complete with the sorrow and regret for previous actions and not only a promise to do better and be better, but a plan as well for how to make that happen. What woman doesn't want to hear that after difficulties? Who doesn't want the relationship of their dreams, especially coming out of the relationship of your nightmares? He vowed to be better, do better, and live better. I have always been an "actions speak louder than words" type of person but for whatever reason, I didn't wait for the actions to follow this time. I didn't need a man that badly; I needed him to be THAT man badly. I needed the man who would finally love, honor, cherish, and protect me. I needed the man who would build a family with me. I needed the man who would be there for me to do life with. And I'm still waiting for that man to show up.

Breaking the cycle is not easy, but it can be done. It all starts with a decision. Everyone can't leave right away. Whether you stay or go, rebuilding your relationship with God will be paramount to your healing. I want to encourage you, no matter how far away from Him you think you are, He is closer than you realize. He is always near the brokenhearted. This story is breaking yours. I repeat, from today forward this is gone. You've read, you've cried, you've prayed, you've heard. It's time. You don't have to do it alone. Find a trauma-informed coach or counselor to help you work through your thoughts and feelings and build an exit plan. Today is your decision day. It's time to make the decision to trade this story for God's story.

LESSON 9
While Riding Through the Storm: Ways to Practice Self-Care During Divorce

I would venture to say that most people do not get married and plan to divorce. I know there are people who go into it saying, "Well if it doesn't work then I'll get one," but in general, most of us are looking for our own special version of happily ever after. For the most part, you know every day won't be rainbows and butterflies but you're expecting that more times than not there will be. Then one day all the "No Year Problems" start to happen. "No Year Problems" are those that should never happen during any year of marriage for any reason, especially at ongoing or consistent rates, such as infidelity, constant bickering and arguing, etc.

Sadly, I found myself attempting to deal with a series of "No Year Problems" very early in marriage, which ultimately led to separation and filing for divorce. The few people that I confided in when I first began the process all had the same question, "How are you feeling?" A lot of times I didn't have an answer for them other than the obligatory "fine" because I hadn't taken the time to really think about how I felt, what I thought, or could potentially think or feel. I really was just "fine." It was just yet another stressful event that would have sent me on the hunt for a new thing to do, except I was now armed with tools to process my feelings. To this day, the one scripture that continues to come to mind whenever I'm asked how I'm feeling regarding the end of my marriage is, "We don't mourn like those with no hope," (1 Thessalonians 4:13). Divorce is a form of death. I go into detail about this in "I Married Him, Now What?" (Not so shameless plug for book #2 😊)

Back to the point. Because I have reached a level of perfection when it comes to deflecting, I made it a priority to institute a few things for self-care as I was, and still am, in fact riding through this storm. (YouTube Yolanda Adams, "Riding Through the Storm." You'll thank me later and you're welcome in advance!)

1. **Take time for yourself**. – This can be hard when you're mom, the only one home, the butcher, the

baker, the candlestick maker. We're all the things to everyone except for ourselves. Make a point to take time out in a day for just you. Play a game, read a book, journal, pray, and reflect, or my personal favorite, do nothing. Whatever you choose, let it be something that allows you to spend time loving on yourself.

2. **Don't deny what you feel.** – A lot of times we want to Wonder Woman Up and be Ms. Tough and Hard but take time to sit with your feelings. Acknowledge them and deal with them accordingly. You do yourself a disservice when you mask, hide, or deny what and how you feel. You will be angry, sad, happy, and almost any other emotion you can imagine and it's ok to have them all. Utilize your circle of safety, a counselor, or a coach to help you, especially if you begin to feel overwhelmed.

3. **Get rest.** – In a combination of a "taste of freedom" and realizing that "it really is just you and them," (your children if you have any), it can become difficult to get rest. You may feel like you must stay up late and wake up earlier all at the same time. There will be days when it seems like your mind just won't turn off. One of the things I decided to do was to stick to a specific bedtime. By doing that, I committed to at

least laying down and doing nothing for no less than 6 hours a night. You can listen to relaxing music or use a relaxation app or YouTube Channel. Also, if you need to and are able, take naps during the day. A power nap is a great pick-me-up and energy recovery method.

4. **Work with a counselor or a coach.** – As I mentioned in #2, you may want to have someone to talk to about what and how you're feeling. While our family and friends mean well, most times they're not trained professionals and although they just want to be helpful, some of their advice can be counterproductive. Coaches and counselors have been trained to walk with you through what you're feeling. Do your research and pray before deciding whom to work with. Coaching is an unregulated industry so while training is helpful, it's not required. Counselors must be certified to practice in the states where they provide services. I will include a list of helpful resources at the end to aid your search.

I get it. Each of these has its own level of "Ugh, I can't do that" attached to it, especially when we're the present parent and most times the sole custodial parent sorting out school whether in-person or virtual, and working full-time, part-time, or anytime. I'm right there with you. What's important to remember, and what I remind myself of daily, is that if I'm not "fine," my children won't be either.

For far too long we were probably in spaces and places that did not allow us to pay any attention to ourselves. In going through this process, it's easy to focus on everyone and everything else. This isn't my entire list, I also pray, read the Bible, and write. You don't have to do them all at the same time. Start with one, work your way through the list, and feel free to add your own things. If you need ideas on how, please feel free to contact me and we'll walk through it together. This is the year and the time that we stop trying to pour from an empty place and becoming burnt out. Instead, we are going to do what is necessary to healthily refill ourselves while we are riding through the storm.

TAKHIA GAITHER

LESSON 10
The Rule to Break

[There is] is a time to tear and a time to mend; a time to be silent and a time to speak.   *- Ecclesiastes 3:7*

E ngaged and married folks, what's one of the top 5 rules you have heard regarding starting your marriage and remaining "happy" in it? Take some time and write them down. I'm sure any of us would have a list greater than five, but I know for me the one I heard the most was "Keep everybody out of the business of your marriage." It's not bad advice. Who really needs the input of people whose opinions are jaded from their situations telling you how to start your married life? Y'all, you and your husband, are supposed to work that out and find your groove. I'm not sure whether I heard it in tandem or I just took it to mean in general, but I also recall taking this stance before I

79

went down the aisle. Had I not taken that position, I could have saved myself years of heartache and pain, but God wastes nothing, and He used it all to put me right in the place where He wanted me to be.

Proverbs 27 talks about the perils of living with a quarrelsome wife. Is that my story? Was I a quarrelsome wife? Absolutely not! The Bible was written for us, not to us. This was a letter from a father to his son, he would know nothing of the annoyance of living with a quarrelsome husband, but I do. And to take it a step further, it wasn't just the quarrelsome husband that I kept quiet about for so long. It was the quarrelsome boyfriends that started this trajectory of dealing with people who said they valued me but then did everything the opposite of that. The complaints were ongoing. Everything was never enough. They tell you they'd like one thing so you do the one thing and then they tell you "Well you should have done ..." Like bruh, really?? At one point in life, I had some choice words that would have followed that question - you can probably guess what words those sentences consisted of. My vocabulary has since expanded but y'all pray for me because some days, le sigh.

Too often we only talk about the abuse we can see. We discuss the violence of being battered because you can see the marks. It is clear and evident that someone needs to be moved to a place of safety. For years I got hit with blows that were seen by no one else and often only heard by me. On the outside, we were picture-perfect, smiling and waving for the camera. Meanwhile ten minutes before in the car, "why'd you wear that?" "You need to wear make-up." "You should have worn this type of shirt." "Why can't you act like them?" But when the car doors opened it was all smiles and hugs and appearances of everything's fine. Fine was far from what I was feeling and was even further from what I really was. I lived behind a mask long before Corona. In fact, mine came off in the pandemic because I'd had enough.

Within these relationships with these quarrelsome people, I should have done more talking. I should have consulted someone I trusted to point out the unhealthiness I was dealing with. I should have consulted a clinician who could have clued me in on the fact that I was dealing with what sounded like an undiagnosed Cluster B personality disorder. I'm not calling anyone anything, I'm just saying, the DSM-V has a list of traits that would deem a person diagnosable with those disorders. However, one of the caveats of a personality disorder is that rarely does the person who is displaying signs of one recognize that they are, so it will be highly unlikely for them to be diagnosed. How do I know this? Because when I finally started talking, after a lengthy conversation with Jesus the first place I went to was to a therapist. He sent me. Which is another thing that goes undiscussed. As a culture, for too many years we have believed that you cannot love the Lord and get your mental health checked out. He made the doctors and gave them the gift of counsel to be able to walk you through the renewing of your mind. If you're questioning your mental state, go get help. It doesn't mean you love God any less, it means you trust Him to work through who's sending you to do what He does best, be God.

The common thread of these relationships is that they were these big exhausting wheels to nowhere. One minute they love you and you're the best thing ever and gushing and glowing and "Yay you." Then out of nowhere, you become the worst person ever at everything all the time, even stuff that has nothing to do with you. Then you're discarded. The silent treatment, the "we're breaking up", the "I'm leaving," (all from them - you're still confused and wondering what just happened), but all the while they're telling you all the stuff you should be doing to win them back.

One day I finally asked, "Who said you're a prize for me to win? I'm not doing this trash. Get a grip." I was disoriented. A shell of me. I looked in the mirror and didn't recognize myself. I've always been quieter, a bit shy, and reserved if you will, but none of that was ever due to a lack of confidence. I'm an introvert, I like to sit back and watch. I was very confident in many things. I made choices not to speak in public or be in spotlight positions but occasionally, God would push, and I would go standing on Philippians 4:13 the entire time because I knew I could do all things because He gave me strength. The day I literally said "I don't know" to having God's strength work and not mine, was the day He swooped in, saved me from myself, and hid me in Him.

Jeremiah 29:11 is my favorite scripture, "For I know the plans I have for you says the Lord, plans for your good and not to cause harm." I was living in harm and didn't even realize it. The more I prayed for help and guidance, the more sermons, slogans, and regular conversations I began to hear about speaking out and not being silent. Having grown up in church, we sometimes get fed "the myth of marriage." I say that because we are led to believe that when we marry our person, there are some things that are just awful but allowed and ok to do because God put you together. And since He put you together, then you would be alright and would make it through whatever those circumstances turned out to be.

Well, I'll be the first to tell you that God didn't put my marriage together, I did. So now what? Even though He gave me sign after sign and signal after signal to not do it, (there were 3 on my wedding day alone), did He still have to honor it? Then came the doubt. The doubt that said if I leave this then I must not be wife material. The doubt that said God will forgive me but He's not going to trust me with anything else because I made a whole mess of marriage and marriage is sacred. The doubt that said I would be this shell of a woman because I left the marriage, all while failing to realize I was already becoming a shell from being in it. What do I do? Do I continue to suffer in silence? Do I get help? Do I just try to do more to be a better wife? What do I do?

The answer was to speak about it. Call those I trusted and let them know what I was experiencing. Enlist the help of a counselor to help me sort through what I was seeing because for so long I'd been told that the very things I saw, I actually did not see. What was going on in my house could no longer stay in my house. It had to leave. I could not deal with it on my own any longer. There is a known response to trauma called fight or flight. In my world, flight meant dodging it, but the fight was a full 10-round bout, and I was ready to get in the ring with Tyson! I had to fight for my mind, fight for my life, and fight for my children. I had to fight for ME! The more I fought for myself, the more I wanted to help others fight for them.

We overcome by the words of our testimonies. One of the biggest lies we hear, and feel is that we're all alone and no one else will understand what we're going through. Or that no one will believe us. But those are all lies. Someone will believe you! Someone is waiting for you to talk so that it gives them the courage to speak out. I am speaking out because it's the story that must be told. Not to make anyone look bad or air dirty laundry. This is not about exposing anything other than the plot of the enemy to destroy God's daughters. If you are experiencing any form of abuse, break the rule. Talk about your house.

TAKHIA GAITHER

THE END ... FOR NOW

I'm a teacher turned author, there are always more lessons, which means there will definitely be more books, blogs, and magazine articles. It's how I teach, how I help, and how I continue to heal, to be honest. We overcome by our testimonies, (Revelation 12:11), and I don't believe I've gone through any of this for just myself. There are others who may have or currently find themselves in any of these situations.

I write for my children - the two I gave birth to, the ones I didn't, the countless that I taught - they're all my kids. Since the day I became a teacher, I've wanted nothing more than to teach my babies well. No parent is ever perfect, and no teacher knows everything but what I do know is that I'm supposed to share so they don't make my mistakes. I want them to do better than me.

It is time to break up with the shame and condemnation that tells us we can't do God's work after going through things. It's time to kill the myth that God wants us to stay in marriages that don't honor Him just because He hates divorce. He does, but not more than He loves the people who are in the marriage. Any relationship that stops you from doing the work that God has set for you to do is not a relationship worth keeping. I know we were taught lots of lessons on loving folks where they are and accepting them for who they are and none of this negates any of that. The reality is that, if you don't love yourself, nothing else is going to matter.

These lessons were my journey back to God's heart and back to me. All the spinning, turning, and twisting, led me right back to the place I should have never left, the Father's arms. As you've started looking at your own lessons, don't let it be through a lens of pity, grief, or shame. Focus on what you've learned and what God has shown you. You may not choose to write a book for the public but keep writing for yourself. Have your own redefining moments.

The Refiner's Fire is hot. It's not easy and it's not meant to be. I'm not perfect but I'm golden! Forged through the fire and, as long as His hand stays on me, indestructible. Until the next class session, I bid you adieu!

RESOURCES

There are a lot of hard things and situations discussed here. I highly recommend getting the workbook to help. Not because I made it but because it will help you sort out your thoughts. Your mind may be spinning, racing, or on 1,000 and it's hard to know where to start. Writing things down helps to come out of that. In addition, I am also including information about receiving assistance in finding help for domestic violence, finding a therapist, and some books and resources that I found helpful and hope that you do as well. You'll be able to access all of that information and more by scanning the QR code below.

TAKHIA GAITHER

ABOUT THE AUTHOR

Author, editor, and writing coach - Takhia Gaither decided during the pandemic of 2020 that there would be no more hiding! To date, she has co-authored over 10 anthologies, 4 of which were Amazon Bestsellers in multiple categories, written and created a Bible Study Workbook – *Be the Overcomer*, written for various online publications, created lined inspirational journals, both yearly and financial planners, and currently maintains two blogs. In the fall of 2022, she will launch the Redefining Thoughts Podcast and YouTube shows.

A native of Baltimore, MD, Takhia is a mother, retired educator, author, editor, and certified Christian Confidence Coach. She holds an Associate of Arts in Teacher Education from Eastern Gateway Community College, a Bachelor of Science in Mathematics from the University of Maryland, and a Master of Science in Information Technology from the University of Maryland, Global Campus. She is currently a minister-in-training and teaches courses for her church and provides tutoring for the youth. When not writing or editing, she can be found enjoying the beauty of her outside office, (i.e. the patio ☺), or spending time with her family.

Writing has always been a hobby, so in 2018 she began her blog, *Takhia the Teacher,* and began writing as a volunteer for the online publication *Godly Today.* She started The Ready Write-Her editing, copywriting, and formatting company in 2019. With the release of her first anthology, *She Changed Her Narrative,* she also became a published editor. Throughout the process of writing, she received countless confirmations that her years of teaching were moving her from public school to the classroom of life. In addition to editing, she is also a writing coach for new authors who seek training and accountability as they prepare their stories for the world to see.

Follow her on the web and on social media:

Web – thereadywrite-her.com

Blog – tsgsgroup.com/redefiningyou

Facebook, Instagram & Pinterest - takhiatheteacher

YouTube - bit.ly/TakhiaTheTeacher

E-Mail – thereadywrite-her@tsgsgroup.com

Editing/Coaching Consultations – bit.ly/TakhiasCalendar

www.ingramcontent.com/pod-product-compliance
Lightning Source LLC
Chambersburg PA
CBHW060337130626
46553CB00003B/1028